MY TALK BOOK FOUR

Complete me Oh Lord and let me release all my troubles; pain.

Hold me and let me feel the closeness of you always.

In all I do Oh Lord I need you, need to be close to you, need to cherish and truly love you. You are my sunshine despite my turmoil and pain.

You are my conqueror; saving grace.
You are my ship
My waters of life
Sail

Michelle Jean

Oh Lord have mercy on my soul and spirit because I truly need to be okay with you in all that I do. And as I listen to **JUST TO BE CLOSE TO YOU by Fred Hammond,** I lift my hands to you in righteousness and truth; praise.

I lift my hands to you and say thank you for being there for me. Thank you for listening to me even on the days I am not contented; the days I quarrel with you.

You are more than a true friend and dear. You are my life and lifeline, my true and more than indefinite all. And as the dreams come I have to rely on you for all I need and more in life.

Lovey it is said, "blessed is the man that walketh not in the counsel of the ungodly" and because I need your blessings of truth and goodness always, let me not falter nor walk in the way of the ungodly, scornful and sinful.

Lovey, Good God and Allelujah you are whom I seek and need, and I cannot destroy what we have because of the enemy and or wicked and evil people.

I have to seek your perfect and true world that is void of all sin and evil; sufferings and pain. But yet as I write, I feel there is something wrong; I write in pain and suffering. I have no happiness in me to continue on with you on this day. I know your world is not like the world of man, hence I have to draw nearer to you; I have to be close to you in all that I do. You are important to me and I cannot afford to lose what we have but yet I want to; truly want to. You are my desire and world so I have to stay close. I have to seek everything from you and in you in a good and true way. Yes I want and need to get closer to you but the spirit is weary; becoming doubtful of you hence the unbalanced and unstable relationship I have with you.

Lovey, listen to the song JUST TO BE CLOSER TO YOU by Fred Hammond because he is right, without you we are lost and you see this globally today. So yes draw me closer to you because I am safe with you but yet weary.

Lovey, as humans we've let you go and look at the state of humanity; living off false hope trying to find you.

Look at the state of our minds; the state of our well being and sanity. We are confused including me.

Look at religion globally and how we as humans kill for a place in hell.

We seek you but cannot find.

We look in the wrong places but yet cannot see that these places are sabotaging us, taking us directly to hell and this is truly a shame. In all I seek, I seek you but yet confusion and doubt surrounds me.

I feel trapped with you.
I do not feel free. I feel like a prisoner with you. As if I am trapped in this jailhouse of no return.

I want to escape these prison walls and find freedom somewhere, someplace away from you, but these prison walls that cage me and take away my freedom are too strong to break, be free of. No one should feel this way, but yet I feel caged like a prisoner with you.

Yes as humans we make mistakes, but lying about it does not solve the problem, it just contributes more to it. It's better for a man or woman including child to admit their wrongs rather than to tell more lies to cover up those wrongs. When you lie you are adding more time on your slate and or plate with death. So no, Lovey I cannot give up on you now that I've found you even though I want and need to. You are close to me and I need to be more than infinitely and indefinitely forever ever without end closer to you. I need to hug you on the days my spirit is overwhelmed by my more than true and unconditional true love of you; thee. Lovey you are more than a beautiful and wonderful friend. I cannot afford to lose you. Billions in humanity has and have lost you and I cannot be like them. I cannot walk on the road of sin because I more than know the beauty and truth of you.

Good God do you know how much peace I feel and get when I listen to beautiful songs such as this.

Lovey, beauty is in beautiful music hence you more than know how I feel about you.

You know me when it comes to you and all that it takes to get to you, I will do it in goodness and in truth. With you I am safe and secure and who would not want and need this for self and others including their surroundings. This is why I tell humanity that true love is rare, and if you are getting goodness hold on to it (goodness) and secure this goodness and truth. But with all this said, I feel like a prisoner with you. I feel trapped; caged because not even my truth and true love of you can break these prison walls down. It's sad that in all that I see and know; I cannot escape your dungeon; cage and trap that surrounds me. So yes confused am I, hence my yoyo affair with you, my bipolar disorder when it comes to you and all that I write for you.

Emotionally I have become unstable in thought, feel and all that I write. Hence I have to wonder if you were ever the right choice for me. I seek happiness but true happiness I truly cannot find with you and in you, hence I truly don't want to stay with you, but I have to honour my word to you. Yes you are a great protector but there's a lot more that I need, hence you need to learn true care and you definitely need to learn about true love. Yes the spirit is weary and the body decaying but this is life when you are a female messenger, you have to take the blunt force of it all.

What I find Good God is that when you are walking on the road to you, you get all the blunt force of evil, hence emotional stability is not thought of all around. Everything is done for you to fail and you see this but yet do nothing about it. Do nothing to calm and soothe our doubtful and distraught mind and this is truly not fair on your part, but a sin. How can one person face so much turmoil day in and day out and remain sane; strong and stable in you and with you?

Your road is a more than a hard road to walk at times, but we have to do it, because the chosen are truly a few.

Lovey no one have to be used and abused. Yes I know we trust the wrong people. Even I at times think you are wrong from me due to my health woes and financial hardships, but I am trying not to look at these because you are more than who I need in my life all around. I know you are securing me and better will and must come; I am just the impatient one because your time is not physical time. Your time is way ahead in the future and at a point and time in time. Thus point and time can be 10 years, 50 years, 10 days, 24 hours from today. Hence your goodness is set at a point in time at that specific time. Yes this is sad for some but this is the way it has to be due to sin; the evils and wickedness of man; humanity globally. **<u>They do not know the more we sin is the further you get from</u>**

humanity. Sin spread and or widens; expand and yes this is why evil do all to control and dominate. The more sin there is, the scarcer you get Good God. I know this but humanity does not. This is why sin has control over man – humanity globally because many things they (humans) do not know. What sin knows humans do not know, hence sin is sin and cannot change for the better, the better good.

Lovey, many things I know hence I know why African Lands, Black Lands had to be conquered. Sin's children had to brutalize us, divide us now look at the black race based on hue and or hair texture; everything. Look at how some blacks have become brainwashed into thinking their skin tone and hair texture is not okay. All that the next race have we want, crave and this is wrong. We have beautiful skin and hair. I truly love my skin tone and nappy ass hair because at night it sticks up to you. Yap, they are my musical and Good God Antenna so no, I have to keep my nappy as pappy hair natural and not do anything to spoil and contaminate it ever again. Well I need to cut it because I truly love low cut hair on me. The combing at my age is so not for me.

So on this day more than ever I truly need to be close to you, so draw me closer to you and never ever let me go.

Yes I see the future.
I see the past.

I see today, but I yearn to see you daily and be with you.

- *You are my pride and joy*
- *My tomorrow*
- *My today and yesterday*
- *You are my all*
- *More than desire*

Lovey I can't stop thinking of you because you are my meditation. So let's connect in a good and true way.

Heal me because I need your healing touch.
Pray goodness for me because I need you to pray goodness for me. My spirit is yearning you; craves you but yet the cage that surrounds me I cannot break and I truly do not know why?

Why is my spirit caged Good God?
What am I missing Good God that I have to feel so caged and broken with you?

Why are you trying to break me?
Why are you trying to kill me?
Why can't I break free of this prison wall?

Lovey, truly pray for me because I need prayer today.

You know where I live so why can't I live with you here in the physical world without restraints and constraints?

Lovey, why can't you touch me each and every day so that I can feel you?

Remember how someone touched my feet (toe) in LA, why can't this be you daily?

Why can't you touch us like this each and every day so that we can feel alive and refreshed; know that you are there? No one should feel caged with you in anyway but yet I do, and this is truly not okay. I need to break free and live. Come on now.

Why can't we find true happiness in you Good God?

We seek you but cannot find and this is wrong. How can we connect with you in a good way if we can't find you?

How can anyone be truthful to you if we do not know what your truth is?

Yes it would be great to have you each and every day, but unfortunately you are truly not there. The earth is filled with too much sin and this is truly a shame. I need to smile a beautiful smile and or put a beautiful smile on my face at the thought of you each and every day and I cannot have this and I truly do not know why.

Truly do not comprehend why you do not want this for me too.

Lovey do you know how joyful humanity would be if we could feel your true and good, gentle and clean touch each and every day?

I more than yearn and crave you but yet at times I feel abandoned by you, and like I've told you, no one should feel like this when it comes to you. You are whom we seek so let us truly find you. Hide no more because humanity; humans are lost right now. Billions are slated for hell and this is so not right. Yes it's the choice we've made because the offerings of the devil is so lucrative that many could not pass it up. But Lovey, can you blame man though?

No, truly look into yourself and the happenings of this world globally and truly tell me if you can blame man for choosing Death over you?

Look at how I yearn to be near you.
Look at how I yearn and crave you.
But with all this said, I truly think you want me to stay your prisoner. **_The spirit craves release. It must connect with you hence the body of man is the jailhouse and or prison cell for our spirit. It is the flesh that keeps us trapped in a world that we truly do not want and need to be in; hence STRESS AFFECT OUR SPIRIT IN A NEGATIVE AND HARMFUL WAY. THIS I KNOW NOW AND IT'S A CRYING SHAME THAT WE HAVE TO CONTINUE TO LIVE THIS WAY._**

Yes I know the spirit of man was to walk back and or come back to you as one; whole, but because of sin our body cannot come back to you with the spirit. Our body has become contaminated; dirty thus the spirit must shed the flesh because the flesh is dirty due to sin. So because of this the flesh has become the jailhouse and or prison cell of the spirit. The spirit desires cleanliness and because the flesh is not clean to the suitability of the spirit, the spirit must seek to flee the flesh by any means necessary. And let's hope I've explained this correctly.

No not on this day with the earth Good God. We live on Earth Lovey but it seems like Mother Earth is the parent. She's a single parent. Yes I know this isn't a great or good example but look at my struggles as a single parent. Look at the struggles of our people from the past until now; this day and tell me if yearning you and can't having you is justified? Go back to TAKE ME TO THE KING by Tamela Mann and hear what she said. She said, "*her heart is torn to pieces, she tired and her options are few. She's trying to pray but where are you? She's all churched out, hurt and abuse, she weak*" and so much more. And like I've told you, no one should feel like this and or this way when it comes to you. Yes I know many pray to Jesus and not you and you cannot help them, but these people think Jesus is you. Some say Jesus is your son. This is why I also tell you that humanity need to know the truth of you. They need to know you are life and not death. <u>You are the upright triangle not the downward triangle come on now.</u>

They need to know that Jesus never existed.
They need to know that you would never sacrifice your children for wicked and evil people.

They need to know that the church is deceiving them and bringing them to hell. We all can save ourselves Lovey and you know this. All we have to do is sin not.

We have to clean up ourselves; we cannot continue to struggle with death anymore. <u>Yes I know billions have acknowledged death hence I tell you provide for your true own and leave death's children alone.</u> You cannot save them (death's children). **<u>PEOPLE WILL KILL FOR DEATH AND YOU SEE THIS GLOBALLY WITH RELIGION ESPECIALLY IN THE ISLAMIC COMMUNITY AND THE CHRISTIAN COMMUNITY. THESE PEOPLE ARE LOYAL TO DEATH AND YOU CAN NO LONGER PROVIDE FOR THEM BECAUSE YOU ARE NOT THEIR CHOICE OF TRUTH. THE LIES OF SIN AND DEATH IS.</u> SO BECAUSE OF THIS, YOU CAN NO LONGER KEEP YOUR CHILDREN PRISONERS IN LANDS AND OR PLACES THEY TRULY DO NOT WANT TO BE IN. YOU**

CANNOT CONTINUOUSLY GO AGAINST OUR GOOD AND TRUE WILL TO PROTECT DEATH'S OWN.

Billions of people have as has rejected you so truly leave them alone. But in so doing, **protect and secure your true own.**

WE SHOULD NOT BE SEEKING YOU AMONGST THE LIVING DEAD COME ON NOW.

OUR SANITY IS AT STAKE AND YOU ARE NOT SEEING THIS, SO WHY SHOULD YOUR PEOPLE CONTINUE TO HOLD ON TO YOU. THE TIME OF DEATH AND OR SIN AND OR SATAN WAS UP IN 2013. SATAN LOST HENCE HIS CHILDREN CANNOT HAVE THEIR NEW WORLD ORDER BECAUSE SATAN LOST DESPITE HIM TRANSFERRING HIS POWER TO A HUMAN. NOT A COUNTRY BUT A HUMAN.

Your children and people should not be punished for the wrongs of man. *Yes we've made mistakes and it's time the DEVIL'S COMMUNITY AND KINGDOMS TO COME TUMBLING DOWN. It is not fair to earth as to what they are doing, nor is it fair to your children and people.* **You birth it all, so WHY THE HELL SHOULD THE DEVIL AND HIS PEOPLE INCLUDING CHILDREN DESTROY IT ALL?**

Some have died seeking you.

Lovey, many died yearning you, praying to you and no help was there for them. Yes you can say they gave you up like Eve (Evening) did and this is the consequence (s) of their actions. **<u>But was it justified?</u>**

<u>Yes I know you were not their god, but now I ask you, what about me?</u>

<u>Are you saying you are not my God, the God that I choose and chose, go to for all?</u>

I suffered Good God come on now. Going back to her and what she did to me. She took you from me; rocked me to the point of brokenness. I lost it all. She crucified me on her cross of death; hence **<u>I will never ever without end forgive her for what she has done to me.</u>** She took you from me and now look at me. Pleading with you for all; more than all, but pleading to you for life; good and true life.

Look as me seeking you and desiring you to just sit at the edge of my bed and tell me you will always be there for me and that you will never ever let anyone hurt me ever again because you know just how much I truly love you.

All I want to hear right now is how much you truly love me. Lovey, how can I go on without you?

Why should this be?
Why should I crave and yearn you so?

Now tell me this, how can I turn to another God knowing what I've gone through with you?

I more than yearn and crave you but yet at times I feel as if I am craving and yearning you in vain. I feel as if I am giving you all of me for naught. I shouldn't have to feel this way with you, no one should, but yet many of us do.

Yes I feel as if you can't handle my truth and more than true and unconditional love of truth. **<u>It's like you are doing to me what humans are doing to you in my book and this is not right.</u>** Each individual love you in their way I guess but I cannot just give you love, I have to give you true and more than unconditional love of truth. I don't know Lovey because I need you and if I have to staple you to me I will. No come on now. If there was a way to staple, sew you, glue you and even paste you to me I would and will. Picture frame wow, wouldn't be good enough for me to contain you and me. Yes mi woulda sidung pan yu tu if it was not unholy, but I cannot sit on you because it's unholy to do so. But if it was okay to do so just to have you right by my side I would.

Yes this is the crazy in me talking now. And don't you dare say ya think because you know I have crazy thoughts such as these for you. **<u>Hence it is not wise to let</u>**

your children go without you. Some of us like me cannot take the loneliness and distance when it comes to you. We want and need to be close to you but you are putting up your defenses and saying woo, woo wait a minute don't come any closer.

Look at how I am trying to do all to secure you and honour you.

Look at how I yearn and crave you TO THE POINT OF INSANITY IN MY BOOK.

Lovey we all need a good and true father and you are that father so stop letting us seek you. IT'S TIME WE FIND YOU AND BE AT REST WITH YOU.

Many, hundreds of millions desire you Lovey, so give it to them. Give these people their desire; You. You cannot hide anymore. You have to open our eyes to you so that we can hold on to you forever ever.

Sin has and have caused many pain Lovey and you know this, so truly help those that need you in a good and true way.

I need you.

I truly don't want to cry for you anymore Lord come on now.

I don't want to hurt anymore because I feel you are not close to me and or truly there for me.

I don't want to go to my bed at nights anymore without kissing you and telling you just how much I truly love and adore you.

I don't want to choose another panty in the store without you giving me your approval.

I don't want to buy another bra or dress without you saying yes those look good on you; fit you perfectly.

I don't want to write another word without you giving me your approval. Every word I write Lovey should be devoted to you and the more than unconditional love of truth I have for you should ease the pain and suffering of our children and people come on now.

Every word of praise I write to you should heal those who read these books including heal me and you.

Every word that I write to you should touch the lives of those who read them and make them strive for a better way; a better way of life in righteousness and truth.

Every word I write to you should touch you Good God and Allelujah because you are My Lovey, more than true love. I need you in all that I do.

Down to my hair I need you to touch and cut. I want and need to cut it and colour it but I need your approval to do this. I value you so much that I truly do not want to make any decision (s) without you. These things I need you to comprehend Good God come on now.

What good am I without you?

I've made you my true life and desire and I don't want to lose your presence. I truly don't want to lose you. Humanity is lost without you and I cannot be like the rest of humanity. I cannot be lost like them. I have to be me when it comes to you. I have to be forever ever true and you know this. So why are you not this way to me?

Why do you let me yearn for you constantly?

Lovey I need you, I need you, I need you. No other god will do. You are my right but yet I feel as if I can't exercise my right with you on some days because of the sins of man that surround earth, you and me.

Lovey, why can't we clean up the sins of man and make earth whole again so that all will be safe from sin and harm; death?

It's not fair Lovey, it's not fair for me and your people to be crying out to you and can't reach you.

Do you not see our tears?

Do you not see my hurt, pain and tears right now?

So tell me, how can your people including me go on when we can't reach you when we want and how we want?

<u>Death's children reach him quickly with their sins, so why can't we reach you even quicker?</u>

Why do we have to hurt and feel pain for you?

Why do we have to feel ignored, as if you don't care?

<u>Yes I want to leave you but not for another god. I can't see myself living a nasty and unclean life with another god. Right now I need a piece of mind.</u> The faces of death are coming again and trust me some are making sure I remember their faces. Like this one younger black lady that's in a pink wife beater like top that hung off her shoulders. She had low cut black hair. Pixie cut would best describe her hair and she was bending over. Her skin is dark and she seemed to me like she was a prostitute and or drug addict. I also saw this young white girl that I would peg to be in her late twenties and ore early thirties. She could be younger. She did not have blonde *hair but light brown to brown blonde hair if that is a colour. She had a pig's snout for a nose. I also saw this black lady with the oddest nose. So yes I am seeing disfigured people again hence I am seeing death before it happens. So you tell me who would not go insane after seeing these things.*

Yes I am seeing death more and more because the waters of earth is gearing up to take many lives as well.

I see myself losing my citizenship card and then finding it.

I see myself flying, taking an airplane more and more.

I see myself reasoning in my dreams and I have to reason with you. BUT LIKE I SAID, <u>**LEAVING YOU I WANT TO DO, BUT NOT FOR ANOTHER GOD. I JUST NEED A BREAK FROM YOU YET AGAIN. I NEED TO REFRESH MY SPIRIT AND MAKE IT CLEAN THE WAY I WANT AND NEED TO MAKE IT CLEAN.**</u> *Losing you is not an option, I just need to find me now, find where I truly belong with you and in you; your kingdom and world.*

In all that I've done, I've focused on you and our people but I now have to focus on me. I need to gain strength because death is slowly killing me and I cannot have this.

I truly need to live even on the days when I truly don't want to.

Wow Good God it's April 09, 2015 and I just got the shock of my life with someone I called a friend. Lovey, someone can be so cold and heatless?

No, can a man be this cold and heartless; without care; feel? Now tell me, is this what it feels like to you? **Is this what void; lack of truth feels like emotionally?**

Lovey, I have to ask because in all that I've come to you with, **are you truly this way; this cold and heartless when it comes to me?**

Lovey, there is this longing there and all that has come into my life, my desire has always been goodness and truth when it comes to them; all that I do for them. My truth has to unconditional, but never in my life would I think he would say this to me. But then again, as my second son said to me earlier this morning, it's not everyone that cares about you in life. If you can't care about me then he does not need them.

Lovey have we become so heartless and cold that the simple and good things in life you are willing to destroy.

Lovey, what have we truly become as humans?

No Lovey I can't believe we've become this heartless and cold towards each other. Hence I have to stop doing because in all that I do it's in vain. **<u>I've learnt that truth and true love cannot warm a cold man's heart; a man that is not capable of truth and or true love.</u>**

Wow because this hurts, truly hurts.

Lovey, Oh my God, I feel the pain in my belly. Man can be this heartless and cold Lovey?

No, I can't get beyond this on this day. I know this should not surprise me but at what stage and or what could be so painful and hurtful for a man or woman including child to be so cold, void of truth and or true love.

Lovey, I have to question you now.
I have to question my relationship with you now.
I have to look at you differently as a person, God and my Truth; All.

Lovey are you this way with me? Void of truth and true love?

Am I wasting my time with you as I've wasted my friendship with him?

I'm sorry Lovey but I have to ask because I am rocked in the true love and truth department.

Lovey, can a man or any human being be this cold and hurtful; painful.

Can a man be this void of love or even true love?

Lovey, feel is important to me when it comes to you. My emotions are important to me when it comes to you but for a man to have this much darkness; void in them wow. Hence I ask you, **what is the point of you or even me staying amongst humans that hath NO GOOD AND TRUE LIGHT FOR SELF AND OTHERS INCLUDING YOU GOOD GOD AND ALLELUJAH?**

What is the point of saving heartless and cold humans that cannot see and gravitate to truth and true love?

What is the point of saving heartless human beings and losing your soul in the process Lovey and Good God?

Dear God things are changing for the worse and I am seeing the worse in humanity more and more and I truly do not want or need to live amongst them. I cannot deal with the coldness and heartlessness of man, hence please help me to find that perfect place where I don't have to deal with any. I cannot live amongst heartless and cold people anymore. I need to be free and rid of them in my life Lovey. ***Also, if you are this cold and heartless let me truly know so that I can truly flee from you and void all my asking of you. I truly do not need you Lovey to be this cold and heartless.***

I cannot want to draw closer to you and you are pulling from me; avoiding me. It makes no sense on my part to hang on to someone and or a God that is not truth; know not truth. Come on now.

Lovey, to truly love someone or something; you unconditionally is more than wonderful. This feeling that builds up in you, you don't want to lose. So why wouldn't anyone want and need truth Good God? Why wouldn't they want and need you in all that they and or we do daily?

Wow Lovey this is weird for me because I don't know how to compute and or take this coldness.

<u>LOVEY; IS THIS WHAT HELL FEELS LIKE?</u> Forgive me for asking Lovey but is this truly what hell feels like? **This**

coldness and heartlessness of man, is this truly what hell feels like?

Wow Good God, truly wow because man truly does not know truth and true love and this is more than a shame.

Now tell me this Lovey, HOW CAN ANYONE SAY THEY BELIEVE IN YOU AND BE THIS COLD AND HEARTLESS?

Anyone that say they believe in you and mistreat, abuse and lie; do all manner of evil and wrongs are a fraud, believe not and know not you Good God come on now.

THEY HAVE NO PLACE WITH YOU THIS I KNOW FOR A FACT. LOVE IS NOT TRUTH, TRUE LOVE IS TRUTH, BECAUSE TRUTH CAN NEVER BE UNJUSTIFIED, NOR CAN IT BE VOID OF TRUTH; BE HEARTLESS AND COLD.

Lovey I need you but I truly do not need the pain of man. I do not need the coldness and heartlessness of man. I need true love hence I need you.

Oh Lovey, why is death shattering my heart. I dreamt I was in this place. This place Lovey was like the center of the world but not our world as we know it. It was the center of a Canadian Province I think, but truly do not quote me on the Canadian Province. This place had to do with water.

<u>In this place no black people reside because it was a vacation place that no one on earth knew about.</u> Lovey, humans know not beauty until they see this place. Like I said, no black people resided in this place, just beautiful white maidens and or girls that circled a particular part of the water. They moved in unison with beautiful and colourful array and the most beautiful flowers were in the water that they moved around. This was not a ritual or anything; this was the way the water was in its natural beauty and flowering; form. While the young girls or maidens of white lineage was in the water, these circular white balls, small as if snow balls came into the water and some began to split as if in half. This lady that was the tour guide (white tour guide) said man knows not of this place and or have never seen this place before. Please do not quote me word for word but it was something to do with this effect man not knowing of this place. Lovey, this place is beautiful and man knows not of it hence, how can I capture this beauty to show man and or humanity?

Lovey flowers grew in the water and these flowers including white females were beautiful but not like human beauty. They looked human but Lovey no beauty on earth comes close to their beauty nor does any earthly beauty come close to their beauty.

After seeing such beauty I went into this place with a white man that was in a grey suit and or grey clothing. Lovey he seemed to be Italian, an Italian rascal that lacked truth, meaning he was a con artist. Lovey he tried to get me into his scheme but I would not budge. Suffice it to say, after all that, there was this dead white man in a casket. Lovey, the man looked worse for wear because in death he was ugly to me. Old in grey clothing with eyes closed and a ugly well slightly crocked and somewhat wrinkly mouth outline. I know this is vague but like I said, he was ugly in death. Maybe because he seemed up there in age; say around 83.

I also dreamt I was in the hospital so I truly have to watch my health closely. Because when I left the hospital Margaret was giving me a this beautiful white and black dress. I truly like the dress but I did not want to take it hence in the dream I did not receive the dress. I fainted in my dream before I could get the dress. Also in the dream I was saying Margaret lost weight. In the dream she lost a lot of weight so I truly do not know what's going on in LA.

I truly do not know what white and black dress of beauty means. I so have to call her (Margaret) and see how she's keeping because she was good to me while I was in LA. So I have to check up on her frequently.

It's still cold and the mood swings are becoming frequent. I feel like I am trapped in a world void of warmth, true care; truth. It's funny the electricity is gone and I feel a sense of loss. So I have to wonder if this is what it's like to lose You – Good God and Allelujah.

It's like there's a void there that cannot be filled.

It's as if a part of you have died and there is only darkness around you even though its daylight; the daylight hours.

Weird by yet true. Therefore happiness never last in my world. Pain and heartache lasts but never happiness. Brokenness is in my world hence suffering last and nothing else. There isn't a sense of peace just desertion, a feeling of loss as if you are lost. Its weird, yesterday, I asked Lovey Good God and Allelujah if he was that cold and heartless to me. I don't know if I angered him in a way but I truly don't know think so but yet I truly don't know.

It's so weird after asking that question not long after out of nowhere lightning sounded at my door – very close outside and it's not like a swift lightning. This one was slow, as if walking slowly because you can feel and hear the lightning walking slowly. It's now the daylight hours and I am thinking about how slow that lightning was walking. Wow. So yes just maybe I angered Good God and Allelujah but I truly do not think so but maybe, just maybe I did. Or he's just telling me in his own way that he's slow to anger, so nice try but it's not going to work.

But with all this said and with my weirdness, why do we have to continue to be lost when it comes to Good God?

Why do we have to feel abandoned?
Helpless

Why do we have to be so poor financially, health wise and spiritually (doubtful)?

No come on now Fam, why do I or you have to doubt him so much?

Why is it so hard to attain him?
See him in human form; face to face?
We're not all dead, so why can't we see him face to face?

It's like no matter how hard you try, he's not there, he's not hearing you and giving you what you need to break down the prison walls that surround you.

Life isn't about doubt and pain, stress and heartache or even fear, but yet I have doubts when it comes to him. I have pain and hurt when it comes to him. I have fears of losing him. This isn't the life I need and want for myself nor is it the life I need and want for you. There's a fine line between me and him hence what am I doing with my life?

What am I doing with your lives?
Am I giving my truth in vain to a god that truly do not deserve it in any way?

No I don't think so but yet I have these doubtful days.

Without him our spark is gone.
We have no light.
We're dead.

Yes many things are happening now and I have to rethink BC, British Columbia because of the oil spill. It's like each way I want and need to go in is blocked. Something bad happens so that I don't go; can't go. Fam, British Columbia is it for me, but yet it isn't from a different angle. Bummer yes but I guess this is the way it has to be. Got to stick with the Cayman Islands. This is where Good God wants me to be.

Yes I am at odds with him Fam because the Cayman Islands does not have enough trees for me. Nor does it have a lot of hills, nor is it mountainous, it's flat. I have to have hills to go up and down; the walk and climb people. I truly love to walk. I know I should not complain because Good God knows best, but I can't help it. He's my good portfolio and he knows best but I can't help it. Hence lost am I because I have no electricity literally. It's like he's gone and I am all alone.

I have no life, no energy. Wow this is a great void. Without him you are doomed, feel doomed.

Without him there's nothing to do, scary but true.

Yes I have many questions now but I don't think I want to ask them.

As I interrupt this book I am sorry the pictures truly cannot be colour. It's April 11, 2014 and this morning I had some really weird dreams. Some had to do with reasoning; talking about truth in many ways with children. And to be repetitive and I am repetitive in these books and don't you dare say ya think, because you know I am. I have to drill truth and true love into your heads for some strange reason. No I should not have to because billions of you know that **"TRUTH IS EVERLASTING LIFE."**

In order for us any of us including me to have everlasting life with Good God and Allelujah, we must speak the truth and do truthful things at all times.

Yes for many it's not easy because some of us have jobs that require us to lie to the consumer and or customer.

Some of us (you) are raised in lies, so all you know are lies and deceit. And it matters not if these lies and deceit are conditioned in you by the clergy and or members of the church via your so called holy bible and books. No book is holy because I've never seen a holy one yet in the living. I've seen Good God's holy book in my visions but I've yet to see one in the living. And truly do not say these books are holy because I cuss and get on bad in them due to my anger and spiritual feel at times. Do not label me or these books. Like I've told you in some of the other books in the Michelle Jean series of books, I'm one to pick up Lovey, Good God and Allelujah and put him to one side and say Lovey I've got this and rib you rude and proper. All that you think will not come out of my mouth will. I do not make joke with Lovey and he knows this. I am more than true to him in every way because down to my underwear I want him to pick for me to wear each and every day. This is the way I am with him. If he could braid or plat my nappy as pappy natural kinky hair that sticks up to him at nights when done a certain way, then YEAH ME.

I truly do not want to do anything without him, but this is not the reason for the interruption in this book. Like I said it's April 11, 2015 and this morning I had some weird dreams. The weirdest one is someone told me Stacy Keibler of the WWE is going to die. Now people me being me when it comes to certain dreams I just laughed. Not laughed but toss them to the side as garbage dreams. Yes this was a man that told me this; hence I ribbed Good God and Allelujah and even called him Good God and Allelujah a liar. No Fam, I am so fed up of the bullshit in the spiritual realm when it comes to men, male spirits that I refuse men. Dem too damn lie. I have no faith or trust in any of them including Good God anymore. *I am tired of them telling me things that are lies hence as a messenger you have to watch out for the men in the spiritual realm with their lying bullshit.*

Remember he, the white man in the floral shirt told me Jamaica and Japan is going to be destroyed. Well destruction has not come has it?

Remember I told you Good God gave me seeds in a brown bag to plant over 100 million acres, and I've yet to receive this gift in the living.

So when men tell me things I can't be bothered to listen and this has to do with the coldness and heartlessness that I am finding in men in the living. More so this than the lies that they tell to get you to lay with them and or have sex with them. Yes this is sad on my part but this is reality, the reality of me at this point and time in my life; as well as journey with Good God and Allelujah. **And in me telling you this, does not mean you are to have no trust and faith in your male guides and or messengers.** I was rocked by coldness and heartlessness and this is why I am this way. **<u>This is only temporary for me.</u>**

When I am rocked a certain way, I write a certain way and take out my anger and frustration on Him God – Good God and Allelujah. This is my way and means of venting on a brutal level and or rocked scale. I have to question Good God and he knows this. This is my way with him and it's not going to change because I've made him my all and strength. <u>I give him my weakness so that he can make me strong and whole.</u>

Fam, I've been through hell and still going through hell. It's me alone but yet in many ways I am not alone. **<u>Some of you are going through hell as well and to me this is not right nor is it just, but you have to know that God – Good God and Allelujah is in the storm with you and he's not going to make you fall</u>**.

<u>You get rocked emotionally so go to him with your heartache and pain like me and or I do because he does deliver.</u>

No problem is too great for him. **<u>You have to know that when you are walking on his pathway, evil tries everything for you to fail.</u>**

Evil rock you brutal and hard but you have to have strength and trust him. Yes you can tell him you don't trust him because he lets things happen to you. I do. And don't think that evil will not use your children to get to you, evil will. As humans we feel, have emotions. **Trust me Good God do not judge you based on your emotions.** **<u>No one can be judged on his true feelings.</u>** If you hate a person you hate a person this is fine. **<u>WHAT IS NOT FINE IS WHEN YOU TAKE UP ARMS TO HURT THAT PERSON.</u>**

When you are down someone will call you or send you an email to make you laugh no matter how perverted that email is. Or you hear that song come on the radio that puts a smile on your face. And it matters not if that radio is a YouTube video. Good God is there despite the way I write when I am hurt. If he Good God and Allelujah is getting truth and true love from us, me and you, why wouldn't he secure us with him and stop the pain?

Why continue to let wicked and evil people tie us and conquer us?

So yes this morning I got down on him and told him he was a liar. To me he truly do not care about his people because if he did, he would not continue to let people hurt them, lie to us and cause us hurt and pain.

If I truly care about you, WHY WOULD I ALLOW SOMEONE TO HURT YOU; CAUSE YOU PAIN? So yes on this day he truly do not care in my book come on now. But yet I know otherwise.

For someone to tell me Stacy Keibler is going to die is beyond me. Why tell me this if you know that the information is wrong and or false? *I know from my dreams that when I see female death, usually it's the opposite; a male is going to die not a female.* **Yes I know I did not see her death, I was told** she is going to die hence I do not put any merit on this. Yes I could be wrong but my spirit does not put any merit to this. **Maybe it's because I am not use to someone telling me someone is going to die. I am use to seeing death before me literally, so this new phase of death means nothing to me because I truly do not know about it.** They are like waking visions, visions I see before me in the waking hours of life. I cannot comprehend them so I do not put value and or merit to them. To me they are not true, they are lies told to me by men in the spiritual realm to keep me satisfied, but in truth I am not satisfied, I am truly disappointed and confused. Confused and I don't think confused is the right word to use, but confused as to why these male spirits would lie to me like this.

Yes I am drawing negative conclusion but until these visions come true then they are lies to me. *(Waking visions and telling visions)*

So yes I am going to leave the Stacy Keibler death alone because in truth this truly does not concern me in any way.

It's so weird because after telling Good God he's a liar I went back to sleep and he showed me something that he's never shown another human being. At least I've never read that he's shown another human being this.

Fam, I truly don't know what he Good God is doing because he showed me in the living that he is slow to anger with the slow walking lightning I told you about above. **BUT FOR HIM TO SHOW ME THE NAMES OF THE PEOPLE IN THE BOOK OF LIFE SAID IT ALL. YES FOR HIM TO DO THIS SHOWS ME THAT HE TRULY AND REALLY TRUSTS ME BUT IT DOES NOT EASE MY PAIN AND HURT; DISTRUST OF HIM ON THIS DAY.**

The Book of Life is not a scroll nor is it a book. It is this long white free sheet and or roll with people's name written in black ink on it. The names of people are in alphabetical order and start from A and go down. I did not see all the names on this sheet and or roll of paper that is as big as the rolls of paper below. And please note; I took this picture from the internet for illustration purposes only and no copyright infringement intended.

Now you know how big the roll is and just what this roll looks like. This is what the names were on. Reading the names the roll was going fast but I could read the names. I can't remember if Al was one of the names but Aiko stuck in my head for some strange reason. If I've spelt the name incorrect and or gave the wrong name I am truly sorry Good God but this is what I can remember. **<u>Yes some of the names were two letters but they were not in English though English characters were used.</u>** And I've told you in some of my other books that no language on the face of this planet comes close to the language of Good God and Allelujah. I only saw names up to A. I did not see the

B and onwards name. And no, I did not see my name Michelle on this list nor did I see my middle and last name. I only saw names up to A and A only. I cannot tell you if these names are the first or last names of people. So please do not ask me if it's the last name or first name because I truly do not know. If these names are surnames then you know that your family's name is in the book of life, but like I said, I truly do not know if it's the first name or surname that are written in Good God's Book of Life; Roll. **_So when people tell me about tribes of Israel I can tell them to sit down because I know for a fact that GOOD GOD AND ALLELUJAH DO NOT DEAL IN TRIBES, MAN DOES. AND YES I KNEW THIS BEFORE THIS VISION AND OR DREAM._**

Good God deal in children. His people are children hence I tell you to secure your child and teach them right; the truth because if you don't, truly woe be unto you. Do not wait until the child is old and or when you cannot bend that child. Yes every child has a mind of their own and many won't take your telling, but you never know in old age after you are dead and gone. Goodness does stick because there will come a point in time when that child remembers the goodness you've done for him or her. Yes the good you've taught them. Do not look at Eve (Evening) and how she abandoned Good God.

Listen, it's not easy to trust God, but you have to because he knows what the future holds. He's shown me many things and they've come to pass. Waking visions and telling visions I know not about so I doubt them. Yes I should have gone directly to God with my doubts and in a way this is my way. I call them lies and I know I should not do that, I was wrong but it cannot be helped on my part.

Did I fail in my journey?

No, because I truly like seeing. Seeing is my knowledge with Good God not telling. My waking visions I cannot put together because I truly do not know how they work. I know they are death but which land these deaths are in, I truly do not know. And yes I've confused you and I am truly sorry for this because I too am confused.

Is it disappointing that I did not see my name including last name in Good God's Book of Life?

In a way yes, but I worry not about this because I know I have the name of Good God and Allelujah already, hence I am the female Lion, Lyon (s). But it would have been nice to see it written in Silver and or white gold if not platinum. Yes this is me being cheeky and spoilt because I am smiling as I write this. But with all this said, why show me the names of people that are in the Book of Life? We are not secure on earth because there is so much hatred and pain all around and because of this I am losing hope and trust.

I don't know people everything is confusing in my head right now because yesterday was a day for me where my head hurt to the point where I was knocking it. These are those headaches that I get where every follicle of hair hurt in my head. They are so bad that you want to die; this is how severe these headaches get. You have no control over them and sleep is so not your say because when you wake up you feel horrible. You feel so sick that you can forget and do forget. For example my first two children went out, and I can only remember one coming back in. Both my children came in, but I can only remember my oldest child coming back into my apartment. Weird. Selective memory I truly don't think so. These headaches are beyond migraines because they are that painful and yes I can over stand, understand and comprehend why people would have suicidal tendencies with this pain because I have. The pain is so severe like I said; that you literally want to die.

Is this stress induced?

Yes to a certain extent, hence stress is a killer, kills the body, mind and spirit all around.

Everything is so stressful that I truly loathe how I'm living as well as loathe the environment I am living in more than infinitely and indefinitely. No one should live in an environment that causes them stress and pain to the point of worse than migraines and loathing. And no matter how much I complain to Good God he does not care, he keeps me locked in prison; an environment that I truly and more than unconditionally do not want and need to be in. So tell me, <u>**how can he show me his Book of Life and let me read the names when I am doubting him, can't even trust him with my well being on this day?**</u>

Am I selfish?

You can say so because he's brought me through the storm in many ways but he's also put me in the storm.

He's put his people through the storm also. HENCE LOVING SO IS TRULY NOT LOVING TRUE IN MY BOOK. LOVE HURTS BUT TRUE LOVE CANNOT HURT INTENTIONALLY.

True love has nothing to prove but love; hate does.

A person that truly loves do all that is good and true to grow with you and build with you not just for today, but infinitely and indefinitely more than unconditionally without end.

True love cannot end, it's true.

True love is care, because true love take care of each other without end.

True love is not sexual gratification nor is it what society thinks beauty is. Humanity knows not true beauty hence humanity knows not true love.

Yes Good God protects me but with my visions and or dreams this morning, none of that means a thing to me.

HENCE I WAS ASKED IF I TRULY WANT TO GO?

AND THE ANSWER TO THAT IS YES. I TRULY WANT TO GO BECAUSE MY TRUE AND MORE THAN UNCONDITIONAL LOVE AND CARE FOR GOOD GOD IS TRULY DIFFERENT FROM WHAT HE HAS FOR ME. AND NO, I DO NOT WANT ANOTHER GOD UNDER ANY CIRCUMSTANCES. I WAS JUST ROCKED THAT'S ALL. I CANNOT LEAVE LOVEY TO GO SHACK UP WITH A GOD THAT I KNOW NOTHING ABOUT. AND EVEN IF I KNOW HIM, ANOTHER GOD, I DON'T WANT HIM. I'VE COME THUS FAR WITH LOVEY, GOOD GOD AND

ALLELUJAH TO LET ANOTHER GOD IN. AND TRUST ME LOVEY KNOWS THAT I WOULD BLAST HIM AND CUSS HIM RUDE AND RECKLESS IF HE AS SO MUCH LET ANOTHER GOD COME CLOSE TO ME.

NO PEOPLE, I WILL NOT HIDE LIKE SOME A UNNU HIDE FROM DI JEHOVAH'S WITNESS DEM. LOVEY KNOW HIS GOOD UP KINGDOM WILL TUN UP RUDE IF IM MEK ANOTHER GOD COME INTO OUR SPACE. FI IM ANGER IS NOT AS FIERCE AS MINE. DESPITE MY WAYS AND WRITINGS IM BETTA NUH LET MI GUH.

People, I know the stench of death.
I know what death smells like on some people.
The odour is so foul that you smell it in the living an mi fi guh tek up datday stench? Hell no.

Stench mi nuh like, so why would I give up clean for stench and unclean? Sometimes we need a break from our surroundings and I need a break, but that does not mean I am to lose sight and focus of Lovey. Hey vacations are there and like I said; my greatest fear is losing him. So no, *absolutely no affairs and or whoredom.* **I KNOW WHERE I AM COMING FROM AND I REFUSE TO LET GO DESPITE MY PAIN. I DO HAVE GOOD**

DAYS HENCE I HAVE TO DO ANOTHER BOOK OF DEVOTION.

I can't be telling you I loathe, more than hate and despise the environment I live in and you are doing all to keep me here. So you truly do not care about me and my well being. I am dying here and want out but you are saying stay. No, you are killing my true spirit and true love of you hence I am beginning not to trust you, so yes I want and need out for more than this reason.

You cannot continue to give death's children and home.

You cannot continue to let them rape and kill the environment and leave all unclean, damage, polluted and dirty for your children. We are not Molly Maid's for the wicked and evil of society. <u>Why the hell should wicked and evil people destroy it all?</u>

Why should we come and fix the mess that wicked and evil have and has created in the first place?

Look at it, I truly wanted to go to BC, British Columbia and live with you, but some jackass, ediat and bleeping greedy moron polluted the waterways of BC, British Columbia. So now I truly can't go there because the environment is ruined. Was this fair to the environment and or coastlines of British Columbia?

No it was not.

So now I have to take British Columbia off my go too and live in list.

Cayman Islands is where you want me to be Good God and I have to stop fighting with you when it comes to there. **LA BUENA VIDA IN GRAND CAYMAN IS THE HOUSE YOU WANT FOR ME AND YOU.** I know it's not a 25 million dollar mega mansion but this is the house you chose.

The 25 million dollar mega mansion I wanted and needed for you is located in Atlanta, Georgia at 490 West Paces Ferry. It's a Mediterranean Estate, but I cannot get this for you due to the lifestyle in Georgia, and when Death talks about sin they talk about the United States of America, so because of this, I cannot give you a home in a dirty and unclean land.

America fight for death hence they spend almost a trillion dollars on war, war machines each year to kill whilst plunging their land and people including economy further and further into hell. You cannot kill for death and expect everything is okay.

I do not know why you chose the Cayman Islands and I truly do not want to question you on this anymore because this is my doubt talking. Yes I know my desire for my homeland but it is not my homeland of Jamaica you chose. You did write in the sky JamaicaF. Meaning Jamaica failed you and you did tell me Jamaica is unclean. So I cannot go into this land, because each time I bugged you about it I would smell roast and or burnt breadfruit. You were and still are telling me if I go into the land (Jamaica) I would go to hell and burn. So I have to stay out. Once you've deemed a land unclean it's unclean indefinitely. Yes Jamaica can come back clean but like I've told you, I do not trust any of them to make the island come back clean.

AS HUMAN BEINGS WE ARE NOT LOYAL. We do crap and or shit to our country without realizing that the sins we do, take us directly to hell. We've forgotten that physical time is not like spiritual time. Spiritual time is further in time and it's the physical that must catch up to the spiritual.

So yes in me wanting to leave you, you can say I am not loyal to my word, but I can also say the same thing of you. You are not truly loyal to me or your people because you continue to let humans destroy it all; the environment and this is truly not right. Why should good people pray to you for GOODNESS AND TRUTH and you abandon them?

Why should we have to now come and clean up their mess; the mess of wicked and evil people and have them continue to live with us so that they can make more mess?

Like I said, we are not Molly Maids for anyone. The environment should not come at a cost when it comes to wicked and evil people that cares not for the Earth and the environment of Earth?

You are wrong hence I tell you at times you are unjust. **<u>Do not ask me if I want to leave you and do not show me your Book of Life in the process because if you cared in the first place you wouldn't be panicking now.</u>**

Take care of truth because truth cannot abandon you. You are doing all for me to leave you because you are hurting me. I am stressed and you're not hearing me and this is why I tell you I more than comprehend why other messengers have and has abandoned you, left you because you only care for death and death's wicked and evil people. And this is why they can do all they want to damage and hurt the earth and your good and true people. I cannot be like you because this is not me. I've told you I want to leave my children and be on my own and I will. They asked me for time because they were stressing rude and reckless and I have given them time.

Death asked for time yes, but in doing so death's children have destroyed the earth. They polluted everything and cause hundreds of millions to die in the process. Now they create weapons to kill and they do kill and you are okay with this. So tell me, how can you say you love us so, when you don't even care; have not truth in your heart? Death went against you, because each child and or tribe of death had a thousand years each to pollute and destroy, tell lies and inflict pain and this is truly not right when it comes to life but you have your reasoning for doing this. 24000 years hath Satan to lie and deceive and we are still not learning. It's not 666 like man tells you but 6666, 24. 666 refers to his 3 daughters who are triplets. They walk in unison and they are never ever separated not even in old age. Man say 666 but yet they forget to add Satan himself to the equation. Yes wrong is wrong and no wrong or one can get right for the wrongs they do. **<u>Yes I know "THE WAGES OF SIN IS DEATH," so why isn't death dying?</u>**

Why is it that it's your people that are dying? Yes disobedience because we take up religions of men and kill self and spirit by. Yes this is wrong on our part hence the brutality throughout the ages for many. But this does not make me feel better, we as humans have to do better especially the black race.

Our children must do better also. We cannot say they are our future and continue to lie to them. Yes I know many want your gift, but it's not many that can handle the brutality of death hence many fail; give up on you because you and or they are not contending with physical wickedness alone, you and or they have to contend with spiritual wickedness, and spiritual wickedness is the deadlier of the two. **When you can walk away from man, YOU CANNOT WALK AWAY FROM THE SPIRIT.**

No one can walk away from the spirit or a spirit because the spirit finds you no matter where you go in the globe; world. No it's not confusing, there's a spiritual force that all spirit is connected to no matter if that spirit is good or evil.

I know the truth of you hence I walk alone. I am sick and these books have many mistakes but I still press on despite my weak and ill health. These mistakes cannot be helped because I did try to catch them all. Yes many may be saying there's help out there. Yes there is help out there.

BUT THE ONE THING THAT WE AS HUMANS FORGET IS, WHEN YOU CALL SOMEONE TO BE YOUR MESSENGER, WE CANNOT TAKE ANYONE WITH US. YOU ARE THE ONE THAT IS ORDAINED, NOT YOU AND SOMEONE ELSE. YOU HAVE TO WALK THE ROAD OF LONELINESS UNTIL SOMEONE IS ORDAINED TO HELP YOU. NO ONE CAN SPEAK FOR YOU EITHER. BUT MOSES AND AARON. IMPOSSIBLE, HENCE I KNOW BETTER.

You cannot show me your Book of Life Lovey and continue to hurt me so. You want a place to live and you've showed me where you want to live but in doing so, how am I going to give you this home when I do not have funds to buy it for you?

I've told you, I do not want or need anyone to come and say, here Michelle I've bought the house for you and Good God. I do not need this because I loathe and despise the entitlement attitude. I do not do to get, I truly love to do, hence I truly bug and grill you so.

Why should someone come and purchase this house for me and you? No. I do not want anyone to say, I bought this house for you and Good God so now my name should be written in his Good Book of Life. Nor should any family member come and say, I am entitled to be in this house because my family did this and this and or purchase it for you and Good God. Like I've told you, I am one to bulldozer that house down and say there you go. I refuse the bullshit of man, hence I am the one to do for you. **_I do not want anyone giving me a dime or a penny to go towards this house. I refuse it and if you go against my wish and wishes then you are truly against me in every which way._** You asked me to do something then help me in a positive and true way to help you, not abandon me and cause me true pain. You are hurting me and you are not listening to me, so truly don't blame me for wanting to leave. **_This is our life and if we cannot live it good and true then we have nothing._**

I do not lie to you, so truly don't lie to me and show me your Book of Life and think this is going to keep me to you because it will not, and you know this come on now.

I value you so much but yet you value not me and your people. I do not do to get from you; I do because I truly care about you unconditionally. I know your pain and suffering, and if you are getting truth; cherish it and take care of it. I've told you this.

You don't want to lose me I get it, but don't hurt me.

Do not tell me to do for you and not give me the tools for success. I am tired of begging you like some dog come on now.

You are my FATHER not my master. You are the Father of all and we should not have to grovel at your feet for anything. Nor should death's children use us as a sacrifice in any way. You know how I am when it comes to the environment, and you should not allow anyone in humanity to destroy it. So no, you truly don't care about what concerns me. **So don't try it anymore because you know when I am gone, I am gone more than indefinitely. It will be forever ever because <u>YOU ARE DISOBEDIENT TO THE ENVIRONMENT AND WORLD YOU CREATED; GAVE BIRTH TO.</u>** You like to see us including earth suffer; lay in ruin and in pain. So truly don't ask me if I am going because you knew eventually I would catch on to you and your lies and leave you.

You want truth but when it comes to truth you cannot truly give it in return. Now tell me, was any of this worth it? Was the pain and suffering worth it?

Look at humanity and this earth and tell me if it was worth it? You gave death a way in to hurt people and humans turned against you. They worship and praise all kinds of demon and or Babylonian idols and deities.

So yes you were wrong in doing this because **LIFE, GOOD LIFE SHOULD NOT COME AT A COST.**

True life is good and true and if you cannot secure good and true life why talk?

Why say you love us so, when hatred is in your heart?

You abandoned life; your good and true people come on now; so don't complain and ask if I want to leave? I loathe and despise injustice. You have to be fair and just and what evil's children is doing is unfair and unjust. You permit this bullshit to happen, so when your children turn against you and accept death, don't cry and panic. No one likes pain, not even you, so how the hell do you expect us to live in pain and suffering and be okay?

No one can be okay. I see death in the sleeping and waking hours and it does do something to your psyche, you know this come on now.

Is Earth deserving of the treatment she's getting from humans? No but yet you permit her unfair treatment by humans. So truly don't because in my book you truly don't care. You heart is as cold and heartless as man, men and women without care.

Is this right of me to say this of you?

No it is not, but I refuse to lie to you when it comes to my feelings and hurt of you. You see the pain and suffering of your children; people and continue to let it happen. So yes you can say I am selfish, but guess what Lovey and Good God, this is not all about me, it's about the environment, your good and true people, Earth and the Universe and You.

Despite your hurt and pain, you have to truly care about those who truly love you.

You have to do for them and this is why I get down on you. We know that evil cares not about us and you can't be like wicked and evil people; cold and heartless people come on now.

We want and need to build good and true with you, so why are you denying us our right and rights with you? Yes you trust me fine I get it, but what about my sufferings; financial sufferings and hardships?

What about your people's financial sufferings and hardships? **_It is going to get worse economically for humanity on a global scale and you cannot under any circumstances let your children and people get caught up in this economic mess._** You are sending your people to the slaughter house of death come on now. We should not be the victims of death. So let death go because **"THE WAGES OF SIN IS DEATH."**

Death's children and people are not your children and people; so let them go without regret because billions did not choose you.

You know me because I am one that truly loves to feed the poor. My heart aches for them. I truly want and need to feed the people of LA and across the globe, you more than know this but yet you don't permit me to do this on a massive scale.

Am I disappointed in you for this?

Yeah!!

I truly don't want and need to go into lands that you don't want or need me to go in. Yes you are protecting me but Lovey really; British Columbia?

And don't you dare let the devil and his people touch Russia and the lands I've chosen for me because them be battling words of epic proportion. And truly don't ask me why Russia because until this day I truly don't know. Maybe my feelings towards them will change when I go there and see, but truly leave Russia, Kenya and China alone. Yes the Southern parts of Africa except for South Africa because I truly don't like this land, due to anger and what the Judas Whites did to Nelson Mandela. Hence no true love is in my heart for the people of this land, the White ones based on hue anyway.

Southern France I claim and Scotland I claim so Good God in all that you do, please reserve and preserve these lands for me in true peace and harmony. Yes I know you will change this but this is you because you know best. I will continue to have hope for my homeland Jamaica but I truly won't hold my breath.

So as I continue on, truly think because no one likes to live in hurt and pain.

No one likes to be lied to and like I said, it matters not to me if you show me the names in the Book of Life. This is not the reason why I look to you. Yes I look to you for all because you are my good and true choice of life, but it does not mean I am to live in pain and financial distress all the days of my life.

Your good and true people are looking to you for good and true life; all just like me and you have to be there for them. Yes I know why you do certain things but the time span of evil is too long for man; humans. Yes everything takes time and like you I gave my children time to find a place, but so far they are not looking but I am. I have to start saving now to get an apartment because I cannot depend on you for this. Yes I know the home you want me to be in but if you are not giving me the tools for success how can I be successful? If you neglect me financially, how can I prepare the home you need of me?

You want and need also, but if I have nothing financially how can I give to you? **<u>Remember you chose the Cayman Islands for us not me.</u>**

You want and need an actual house and you showed me the house that you need and that house and or home is La Buena Vida in Grand Cayman, Cayman Islands. You have your reasoning for this land and I cannot go against you because this is what you need. I am trying to give this to you but like I said, I do not have the financial means to do so. So if I fail to acquire this home, then you cannot blame me for failing you because I did try.

I did go to my BLACK OWN and got shot down.

I did try in LA and I saw the selfishness of my Black Own based on hue.

I did try in Canada and got shot down. I've seen and encountered anger with my Black Own. Hence I've told you, people will kill you for the truth and or the lies they believe in. No one wants to hear the truth; hence they bask in lies and tell lies and I cannot do this. The Black Race had their true identity and language taken from them and now look at us, spreading lies and deceit (Religion) for the devil. We've become the devil's slaves and pawns that kiss his feet and praise the death he's given us. Death that they say is good food and we as fools, foolish black people refuse to learn that all that they tell us **IS KILLING US.** Hence I truly do not know what to do. I've come to you for help and you are ignoring me. I do not know another way and I refuse to walk on the pathway of the devil to get you your good and true home. I told you I can build you your good and true home in my heart but you do not want this, you want and actual home for you.

I cannot preach to you or talk to you anymore because I do not know what other avenues to take, and no matter how I try with my Black Own it's not working. I've got wrong numbers and some if you don't put out sexually with some they refuse to help you, and I refuse to lay with anyone to help you. I will keep going until I can't go anymore come on now.

Yes more destruction comes because Earth must be vindicated and she's gearing up to swallow many lands and you cannot blame her for this because she's felt the pain of man; humans for far too long. You cannot charge her for sin either because in all that she does now, it's our fault. **We as humans caused this on self due to our sins.** *The wages of sin is death and we know this, but we do the opposite by continuing in our sinful ways whilst thinking YOU GOOD GOD AND ALLELUJAH SENT YOUR SON TO DIE FOR THEM SO THAT THEY WILL BE SAVED. And I will ask again, if the lie did not work for Eve (Evening), how can the Jesus lie work for us and or anyone in this day and time? Eve (Evening) disobeyed you. She went* against your order and accepted sin. **WHEN SHE DID THAT OR THIS, SHE DIVORCED YOU. SHE WAS NO LONGER COVERED AND OR PROTECTED BY YOU.** As humans we know this but do the opposite.

WE FORGET THAT WHEN WE LEAVE YOU, WE OPEN THE DOOR FOR ALL KINDS OF BRUTALITY.

WE FORGET THAT willful SINS CANNOT BE REDEEMED. EVE (EVENING) FOUND THIS OUT THE HARD WAY. **SHE FELT PAIN, TOILED IN VAIN AND PAIN AND DIED IN PAIN. NOW SHE SITS AT THE GATE OF HELL RECEIVING HER DISOBEDIENT AND WICKED CHILDREN; OWN.**

I know for a fact that you would never ever send any of your children to save and die for wicked and evil people.

You are the giver of life, why would you become the taker? You did not take life from humans; humans took life from self with their sins; the wickedness and evils they do on a daily basis.

You are the Breath of Life, why would you take LIFE FROM THE BREATH OF LIFE; YOU?

Yes I forgive you for her, but in truth, I truly don't want to forgive you for my hurt and pain and I don't have to. Yes I know some of your children live in the belly of the beast, the United States of America but I truly don't want to go to New York and take none out. Yes I am thinking of my LA experience and how selfish and self absorbed some black people are. **You keep trying with black people and we are the ones to fail you, sit in our predicament and praise death over you.** We don't want to get out of our situation (s) and this is so sad. Yes this is my view and my view is correct because I can point to our history (the black man history) over time. **WE FAIL TO REALIZE THAT WHEN WE DISOBEY GOOD GOD AND ALLELUJAH WE DIE.** HE GOOD GOD AND ALLELUJA LEAVE US TO THE CHOICE WE'VE MADE AND A PRIME EXAMPLE OF THIS IS EVE, ETHIOPIA, EGYPT, THE UNITED STATES OF AMERICA, THE CARIBBEAN+.

As blacks we fail to see this and when the truth comes many are doubting like me. **Good God and Allelujah cannot go against your will; the choice you've made and this is why the world is in such a mess.**

We keep choosing death over him Good God and Allelujah and fail to realize that when we continue to do this, death comes on a massive scale and take by any means necessary.

DEATH HAS 24000 YEARS TO TAKE ON A MASSIVE SCALE. THE TIME OF DEATH OR SIN BECAME DUE AND OR WAS UP IN 2013. NOW DEATH MUST TAKE ON A MASSIVE SCALE BEFORE 2032. And I've told you this in some of the other books in the Michelle Jean series of books.

The truth is here accept it because I was set to fail by her. I was to die, because death commissioned my death long before I was born.

I was to toil in vain.

I was to doubt and question Lovey, Good God and Allelujah.

You don't have to because the truth is before you. Do not continue to walk on the wrong road. Billions are slated to die and this is because of our choosing.

Yes you can say I am a fraud and an idiot.
You can call me foolish too.

You can use all the cuss words you want when it comes to me. This does not bother me and you know why?

Why you are asking?

I've done my job, the job GOOD GOD AND ALLELUJAH REQUIRED OF ME. I DID NOT FAIL HIM; I WROTE HIS BOOKS GIVEN WHAT I SAW VIA DREAMS, VISIONS, WRITINGS AND TEACHINGS.

Yes I can stand up and say I came to my own and they refused to listen; refused these books. **TRUST ME THIS BOTHERS ME NOT BECAUSE THE DEVIL DID HIS JOB WITH THE BLACK RACE AND THAT IS SECURE THEIR SOULS, NAME AND NUMBER INCLUDING SPIRIT IN HELL.**

He the devil gave them religion and look at what religion has and have done to our state and mind, earth and well being.

HENCE HELL IS FULL OF BLACK PEOPLE AND RECRUITING MORE. (Islam)

This is how I saw it and this is how I am relating it back to you. **AND YES THIS IS WHY NO JEW MUST FORM ANY ALLIANCE WITH THE ISLAMIC KINGDOM. WE ARE FORBIDDEN TO DO SO. ISLAM IS SPIRITUAL DEATH, I KNOW THIS AND THE TRUE JEWS KNOW THIS. HENCE A JEW CAN NEVER EVER MARRY ANYONE IN THE ISLAMIC KINGDOM OF DEATH.**

Yes you can say I am spreading hatred. So utter those words and let GOOD GOD AND ALLELUJAH BE TRULY AGAINST YOU AND TAKE YOUR NAME OUT OF HIS GOOD BOOK OF LIFE. I will never spread hate and if you say I am then you are saying Good God and Allelujah is spreading hate. This is how I saw it and this is how I am relating it back to you, hence **GOOD MUST SEPARATE FROM EVIL AND LIVE AS PSALMS ONE TELLS US TO DO.**

We are not to go into the congregation of the wicked and evil; defiled. (Churches, Mosques, Temples, Synagogues and what have you that they call holy). He Good God and Allelujah cannot say; I disobeyed him in these books. I told him, I need to tell the total truth and I will not lie for him. I refuse to lie for him or anyone.

I cannot change you from your belief, no one can. You are the one to change you for the better if you want better for yourself and your family. **ABSOLUTELY NO ONE CAN SAY GOOD GOD AND ALLELUJAH GAVE US RELIGIONS OF MEN TO KILL SELF AND SPIRIT BY.**

Anyone that tells me God is a Christian and or a Muslim and or an Orthodox this or that, I can laugh at and say, if God, Good God and Allelujah was a religion, what religion is He?

If God, Good God and Allelujah was or were a religion, what religion does the earth and universe practice? Yes I can see the universe laughing and holding his stomach literally right now.

If God, Good God and Allelujah was a religion, what religion does the animals, trees and waters of the earth practice?

So none can tell me bullshit about God, Good God and Allelujah when it comes to religion or what have you. **I DO NOT HAVE A NEED TO BELONG WITH DEATH; YOU HAVE A NEED TO, HENCE YOU PRACTICE RELIGION.**

I do not need death you do.

I know what death can do, you don't.

I've done my best to tell you and show you in these books. So yes, if the Black Race or any race globally stand against me, Abaaaay. I truly don't care because I've done my job and that is, give you the total truth as it's given to me.

<u>I do not hate myself, I truly love me; hence I do not practice religions of men anymore.</u> I know where I stand in the universe and I know where I stand with Good God and Allelujah. And despite my way with Lovey and Good God, he knows I still more than unconditionally more than truly love him with every ounce of truth within me. My true love of him defies the truth of this world and universe. Our relationship is our relationship not yours. You need to develop a good and true relationship with him for yourself. **<u>AND LIKE I'VE TOLD YOU IN SOME OF MY OTHER BOOKS, IF YOU DOUBT ME AND OR HAVE ISSUES AND OR RESERVATIONS WITH ME AND THESE BOOKS, DO NOT HESITATE TO GO TO GOD, GOOD GOD AND ALLELUJAH AND VOICE YOUR CONCERNS.</u>** Go to him with your truth and true feelings; emotions. **<u>He will not judge you or sin you for this.</u>** I go to him with everything and it's going to stay this way more than indefinitely. Even when it seem like I don't go to him with all, I go to him. So if you feel as if I am an idiot, say Good God this idiot or dutty gyal wey no ha mannas sey this, this and this and I don't trust her. I think she's fake, a fraud and liar. Trust me Good God will answer you.

AS HUMANS WE OPEN THE FLOOD GATES FOR ALL MANNER OF EVIL TO RAIN DOWN ON US.

And don't you dare say this is not true. I am going to interrupt this book again. It's April 14, 2015 and this morning I had some weird dreams but what else is new with me. Remember I told you above I was asked if I wanted to leave, leave Good God and Allelujah and I said yes I wanted to leave? Fam, si how God, Good God show mi my life if I left him. Mi nuh noa but this thing, black thing like a black blob, no before I saw this thing; it was like something was possessing people's body. White people not black people. (White Males)

It's like invasion of the body snatchers but in spiritual form; hence I have to talk to you in depth about spiritual possessions. Hopefully soon. After this possession, this thing, black thing like blob came atop of me because I was lying down. People this thing had strength and it was trying to possess me but I had enough strength to push him and or it off me so that it would not possess me. Now people I don't know if it's the coffee and

Timbits I had before midnight that caused this, but I truly don't think so, because I've had coffee later than this before as well as eaten later than this before. And for you who are wondering, the strength of this thing and or black blob like things is like when someone or something is holding you down in your sleep. And yes I know this is Good God's way of telling me, if I leave him I will become possessed by this thing. **_Meaning people and family, when or if I leave him Good God I am going to die. I would have given myself over to death to hurt me more brutal not just on earth but in the spiritual realm also. He's also showing me, if I walk away from him, I will not have his protection nor will I be under his protection anymore. Like Eve (Evening) I would have divorced him; so worse brutality will come._**

As children we cannot leave his fold because we are married to him. And to repeat myself from another book, the VOW THAT HUMANS TAKE WHEN THEY GET MARRIED IS NOT FOR THEM, IT'S FOR GOOD GOD'S MESSENGERS AND OR CHILDREN. WE ARE THE ONE TO TAKE THIS VOW WHEN HE CHOOSES US. WHEN WE

SIN, WE LEAVE HIM; PART FROM HIM AND OR DIVORCE HIM. *And yes this is why some messengers die brutally at the hands of man; humans. This is also why many blacks have faced slavery and the brutality of slavery by wicked and evil people. Thus I tell you and Good God that my greatest fear in life is losing Him Good God and Allelujah.* Eve (Evening) was married to him (Good God), because she could speak directly to him and see him. This too with Adam according to your Illuminati and or Free Mason book of death; your so called holy bible. Yes it was a Free Masons that commissioned this book to be written because King James was a Free Mason, Illuminati in this day and time. They are all the same because they perform blood rituals. They must sacrifice someone in order to keep their place with death; hell.

No, don't, truly don't, you just don't know. The same nastiness they practice and partake of and in you do it also. Many of you are cannibals literally. (THE BLOOD AND FLESH OF CHRIST). Nasty ass.

So according to your nasty book of the dead, your so called holy bible, Adam and Eve knew God and talked to him directly. When they sinned they divorced Lovey, Good God and Allelujah and were kicked out of His garden more than indefinitely. And yes we do the same thing today when we sin.

WE FORGET THAT THE DEMONS OF HELL CAN USE BY ANY MEANS NECESSARY TO BREAK US AND THEY DO; HENCE OUR OWN SOLD THEIR OWN INTO SLAVERY. YES SACRIFICED THEIR OWN. HENCE THE MANY RELIGIONS OF SIN AND MAN GLOBALLY.

Humans have forgotten that the devil and or Satan have his own race of people (the Babylonians); hence there is war and strife between good and evil.

Good has forgotten as well. **WE'VE FORGOTTEN THAT WHEN YOU ARE UNDER THE PROTECTION OF GOOD GOD AND ALLELUJAH NO WEAPONS FORMED AGAINST YOU SHALL PROSPER.**

WE'VE FORGOTTEN THAT WE ARE TO LIVE AS PSALMS ONE AND COME OUT OF WICKED AND EVIL; SINFUL PLACES AND LANDS. WE ARE NOT TO COMMUNE UNDER ANY CIRCUSTANCES WITH WICKED AND EVIL PEOPLE; SINFUL PEOPLE. THEIR GOD IS NOT OUR GOD; HENCE GOOD AND EVIL MUST MORE THAN INFINITELY AND INDEFINITELY STAY SEPARATED AT ALL TIMES FOREVER EVER COME ON NOW.

We've forgotten that evil is but for a time and once the time of evil is up you are free to roam. Not immediately because freedom takes time to come once you are released from the clutches of sin.

As humans we've forgotten that when we disobey Good God via willful sins WE WILL NEVER EVER GET BACK INTO HIS KINGDOM BECAUSE WE WILLINGLY DISOBEYED HIM LIKE EVE (EVENING) DID. NO AMOUNT OF PRAYER OR SACRIFICE OR LIES OR TRUTH CAN OR WILL GET YOU BACK INTO HIS FOLD; REALM. NOT EVEN YOUR SO CALLED JESUS CAN HELP YOU COME ON NOW. Jesus cannot petition for you, I can't petition Good God and Allelujah for you. Like I've said, IF I AM THE SAVING GRACE FOR HUMANITY, I WILL NEVER EVER SAVE ANYONE THAT IS WICKED AND EVIL BECAUSE WICKED AND EVIL PEOPLE KNOW WHAT THEY ARE DOING. Hence many sell their souls for profit due to greed. Innocent lives were taken hence the sacrifices that humans do can never stop. BUT SHORTLY IT WILL BECAUSE ALL WICKED AND EVIL SOUL; HUMAN AND SPIRIT MUST GO DOWN TO HELL TO BURN AND DIE. SO IF YOU ARE NOT RIGHT WITH GOOD GOD AND ALLELUJAH; TRULY WOE BE UNTO YOU BECAUSE YOU ARE GOING TO DIE LITERALLY.

You don't have to trust or believe what I've written, <u>but you must trust Good God and Allelujah unconditionally.</u> HE'S BEEN TRYING TO SAVE US AND WE ARE THE ONES THAT ARE REFUSING HIM. We are the ones telling him we do not want saving with our sins. When we sin we die. So stop sinning and save yourself.

We all can save self we just have to want and need to. **_Yes billions are locked out and to say my child or children will save me is a lie._** Not every child truly loves their parent. Not every child was raised right by their parent or parents. **AND MORE IMPORTANTLY, WHEN YOU SELL YOUR SOUL TO THE DEVIL AND OR SATAN, YOUR CHILD AND OR CHILDREN BELONGS TO SATAN ALSO. YOUR CHILD AND OR CHILDREN CANNOT BE SAVED NOR CAN THEY SAVE YOU BECAUSE SIN, SATAN, THE DEVIL AND OR DEATH OWNS THEM. THEY BELONG TO HELL JUST LIKE YOU. YOU AS A PARENT SACRIFICED THEM TO DEATH; HELL.**

And it's not oh my god, you sold your soul hence giving death everything that you own and or have including your children. And it matters not if the child is adopted. Hence I truly don't want to be any of those nasty mothers that sell their children to be raised by another woman. Truly woe be unto your asses because **IF ANY OF YOU THINK DEATH AND HELL ISN'T WAITING FOR YOU, TRULY BETTER THINK AGAIN.** WOW WHEN IT COMES TO YOUR HELL. If you know you cannot raise a child and or children then have none because no child is guaranteed to save you. So truly good luck to the lots of you literally.

Yes I know some of you are not capable of raising your children, but give that child to someone that can. No money should be involved. Secure a good and true home for your child and or children in this way, and don't want them back after they are grown. You gave up all right and rights to this child and or your children so leave them alone. Once you've given up your rights to that child; no judge in the physical realm and spiritual realm can give you back that child and or your children because they truly do not belong to you. And don't come here with the biological bullshit. You gave up your rights and legal rights willingly to that child, hence you gave up all biological, legal and spiritual right and rights to him or her; them. Never sell your child. **You are not cursed if you do not have children or do not want any come on now.** Man tell us crap and it's time to stop listening to the crap that men that has not our best interest at heart tell us.

And although I blame Good God I know He did not cause any of this. But I still blame Him in some way because none of this had to be. He had no point to prove to Sin or Death; Satan.

He had no point to prove to man either. He is God and God alone. No one should have to bow to the evil will of man wicked and evil demons that plague the earth. Yes this is hypocritical of me by me saying this because I am contradicting myself, but it matters not to me on this day. He Good God let the lie continue and this is sad. So yes, He Good God is to blame in some way in my book. He should not have given death and or sin and or the devil 24000 years to wreak havoc on man and the earth. The earth did not deserve this. ***Yes I know, just as He allotted the Devil and or Satan time, I allotted my children time. Yes the time span is different and yes they (some of my children) went back to their nasty and dirty ways.*** <u>***They have not learnt anything, so it's the same with MAN; HUMANITY AND GOOD GOD BECAUSE IN TRUTH, GOOD GOD DID GIVE US AS HUMANS TIME TO AMEND OUR NASTY AND DIRTY WAYS AND WE HAVE NOT DONE SO. So yes I see his dilemma also.***</u>

But with all this said, he should have never have allowed the black race and or any race to let the devil in under any circumstance (s) but He did anyway. So yes He's at fault also and don't you dare tell me about will either. Yes He gave us a choice and man; billions of humans have and has chosen sin and evil; greed over Him. Yes I am greedy but I am greedy for HIM and all he has and I cannot change this. I will be forever ever greedy for HIM. But I cannot take the lies anymore hence yes I want and need to walk away from HIM.

He's tried. He's given the black race a way out and we refuse to take it, so leave them the hell alone Good God. *We as black people cannot say He Good God and Allelujah has not tried because he has; we are the ones that keep leaving the door closed instead of opening it to receive our goodness and truth; blessing and blessings.*

We are the ones to constantly disobey and when we get brutal beatings we cry to Good God and say; <u>THE DEVIL IS UNFAIR.</u> WELL IF WE DID WHAT WE WERE SUPPOSE TO DO, WE WOULD NOT SAY THE DEVIL IS UNFAIR AND WE WOULD NOT GET BRUTAL BEATINGS.

We keep walking in the traps of sin instead of leaving those and or these traps alone.

We know the traps are there and they hurt even kill, but we refuse to listen and leave these traps alone.

Some of us, Good God and Allelujah has and have taken us out of these traps, and instead of staying out, we go right back into the mess. So whose fault is it when we get battered and abused even confused? And no in a way I cannot say this for me, I am in a learning phase where I have to go through hell to teach you. Every messenger of God; Good God and Allelujah has gone through this, I am no different. I know this but yet I still complain. Listen in order for you to know you have to see and feel, and I've seen and feel. <u>I am going through it, so that later</u>

on when the harvest comes, you don't have to, but I cannot do it alone. I need these books to reach the right people so that I can start building Good God's kingdom here on earth for his people. He Good God wants a home and I've told you which one he wants. It's up to you now to help me build him; Good God and Allelujah. You have the mandate of death which is before 2032, but we as Good God's children and people cannot wait until it's too late. We have to start acquiring and building now because many lands are going to be destroyed. The sins of man globally has and have gone on for far too long; hence DEATH MUST COLLECT HIS AND HER MASSIVE PAY.

I am also learning about coldness and heartlessness. I've learnt a man or woman including child that have not charity, a good and clean heart; cannot be saved because they have no good will for anyone or anything. Gratitude and thanks is not in them and this is a total shame. Hence I truly do not want people like these in our kingdom Good God and Allelujah. Yes our kingdom because you know that I am not going to leave you stranded, but I truly want to leave you because of lies and nothing else. I am tired of spiritual lies; spiritual wickedness. I am tired of the confusion in the spiritual realm. This has to stop for our people's sake and mine.

Clean hands and pure heart Lovey you know this, so spirits should not lie to me in anyway. Nor should they lie to anyone for that matter come on now.

Yes I know things take time with you, but it should not have to anymore because these are the final seconds of man speaking from a spiritual perspective. Hence years in physical terms.

<u>The crack is in the earth and the earth must open up and devour man; humans literally.</u> These things I should not tell you because I know the pain you feel. Billions are going to die and it could have been avoided; but humans did not choose you. So you have to let things be; give humanity their hearts desire; wish.

Listen, I found a wonderful song by Romain Virgo that sums things up in a way. The song is called, **<u>STAR ACROSS THE SKY.</u>** You are your true people's thoughts and dreams. You are the one we are looking to for a better and brighter tomorrow and yesterday. A brighter and better tomorrow and yesterday that is void of all sin, tears and pain. We've come thus far from then until now; but we cannot give up. I cannot walk away from you though I want to at times because of the unjust and unfair treatment of man; humans and spirits. The time for sin is over, so let it be truly over indefinitely more than forever ever. Your children do not need to face the hardships of man anymore. Look at where I am living. I pay so much for rent, now I am hearing they want us to pay for hydro. **Lovey many of us cannot afford this extra expense; hence I know it's a matter of time before TORONTO BECOME LIKE LA when it comes to homelessness.** *We have homeless here, but there will be more homeless on the streets of Toronto soon because the iniquity of the Amorites; the greedy blood sucking vampires that suck the life and wealth out of people is not yet full.* People are struggling as it is Good God come on now for this to happen! You know I cannot afford this added expense because I am living on a limited income. So tell me, where is the justice in man if man; humans live for greed and are greedy?

Now tell me, are these unjust and greedy vampires the ones you want me to save if I am the saving grace of and or for humanity? If it is, then I say unto you, you are truly unfair and unjust like them. You are not a god of truth but a god of lies and stress; death.

Yes I know the destruction that will be on earth real soon and I cannot stop this, nor do I want to stop this because **"THE WAGES OF SIN IS DEATH,"** and man – humans did forget this; ignore the truth that was given and told to them, so let them pay.

Do not listen to their cries. Just as how they did not listen to you, truly do not listen to them, but save and provide for your true own. Those that truly love you and care about you, save them because they are your true people.

It's April 12, 2015 and I dreamt Fred Hammond. *(Don't say it because by now if you've read any of the other books in the Michelle Jean series of books you should know that I toggle between dates sometimes. Yes a lot and don't you dare say ya think).* *He came to Toronto, so I have to check concert dates to see when and or if he's coming to Toronto. I truly have to meet this man because he's got the singing voice I need all around. In the dream he was dressed in black and I do not like the fact that he was in black. But I got to hug him and I was rubbing the back of his head. Lovey in the dream he was so cuddly, wow. So yes, hopefully one day I will meet this musical genius that soothes my soul and spirit in a good and clean way.*

I also dreamt this white boy. He must have been about 12 and or a little older. It looked like he had no parents and it was as if he was homeless. He was sitting on this bed; mattress that was burnt. It had caught fire from the looks of it. Lovey this boy had eyes that looked grey to me and I think he was in light blue clothing (pants) and I think white shirt, but do not quote me on the clothing. I was more absorbed with the metal railing bed and burnt mattress he was on. The room looked like an attic and he had this box at the end of the bed where he put the garbage of the food he eats in. Lovey, wow because the shaving looked like orange peel and potato peel, but then again it was garbage. Lovey, in the dream he was telling someone, a reporter how he was so tired and he had the stove on and he fell asleep due to tiredness and the house caught fire. But in the dream the fire did not burn him. He had protection from his dog. His dog saved him from being killed. And it's weird, in the dream you could see this white toilet and I think there was this writing on the toilet seat. When you lift the cover you could see this writing but I cannot remember what the writing looks like or what it said, because you could barely see it.

Yes I know this is a weird dream; hence I know I have to address certain issues with you when it comes to children because I am seeing them more and more. Homelessness is an issue also because this hits home, and or homelessness is close to me. No one should be without a home, but yet billions globally are without one and it's a crying shame. <u>Man spend lavishly without thinking of the poor, hence I cannot truly think of the rich man that has not charity.</u>

His charity is to spend and live lavishly whilst buying hairy motels. So in death, I truly hope their lavish lifestyle and hairy motels do for them; save them. <u>And no I am not saying you cannot live lavish, but if you can afford to help the homeless and or less fortunate think of them and help them. Have charity for those who truly do not. This is where some of your blessings lie. Do not wait until your</u>

spirit leaves the flesh, do it now. There are many homeless in LA, so if you can afford to feed one family by spending $10.00 per day then do it because $10.00 per day is all you can afford. **Do not give what you cannot afford. And yes good clean prayers by you is considered giving come on now.**

Lovey as humans we say children are the future but how can children be our future when we screw them up royally and take away their future from them?

How can children be our future when we LIE TO THEM AND CONDEMN THEM?

Lovey as humans', adults use children to do their wrongs and you cannot be okay with this. You cannot let adults and yes some children continue to deceive and mess up their own.

NO CHILD CAN HAVE A FUTURE LIVING IN LIES. ABSOLUTELY NO ONE CAN. If you teach lies and raise your child and or children in lies, they will grow up to be liars and thieves. They will do all that is ill because that's all they know to do.

No one can say they truly love their children and raise them in lies come on now. As adults we know better, so we have to do better.

Yes I've called you a liar and yes I know better, but I have to call you a liar given what I've seen. The dream of Stacy Keibler threw me over the edge and I had to call you a liar. This dream made me want to leave you because to me this dream is a lie. Yes the dream has not manifested but like I said, this dream did it for me when it comes to spiritual lies.

I truly don't know anymore Lovey because I am being rocked this month when it comes to everything; especially the heartlessness and coldness of man; humans.

So yes I am glad I come to you in this way. So no matter how hopeless and doubtful I get, I have to lash out at you and come back to you.

Michelle and Michelle Jean

So as I move forward and regain my composure and put my trust in you, truly think Lovey.

You are God alone we know this, but you cannot continue to let your people suffer like this. We will get fed up and walk away from you and billions have.

Remember the Twitter pictures I've seen.

Remember the Twitter picture of the little black boy being gassed by a white man.

Remember slavery; how we the black race was sold into slavery by our own and others.

<u>Remember the little yiddy black babies that were fed alive to alligators in the American South. Truly remember them Lovey because I've asked you, did you not hear the cries and screams of these babies? These were babies and you made them suffer reckless and rude.</u> Hence the hearts of man is wicked and vile; more than heartless and cold in every way. Thus I cannot comprehend you in many ways. I cannot comprehend why you would let this happen to babies. Yes I know many are not your children because many have and has chosen death for self, family and children over you and you cannot interfere. **But Lovey, these were little yiddy biddy babies. Did the tears of these babies not jerk you, tug at your heart and navel string? Did you not shed a tear for them? Come on now.**

You did nothing to save them Good God come on now. You did nothing to save them, so how can we truly trust you? **Yes I know as Blacks we've turned against you and given you up.** We were the ones to choose false gods and idols over you and because of this, you have to step aside and let the atrocities and brutal beatings happen, but these were black babies Lovey come on now. What child or baby deserved and or deserves that?

What human being or animal deserves that come on now? But yet you permit it to happen and still with all this said, **THE BLACK RACE BASED ON HUE**

CANNOT LEARN TO WALK AWAY FROM SIN AND EVIL.

You tried and failed because we refuse to listen, hence we caused you to fail. Yes I know you cannot fail, we are the ones to fail you and self and we have failed.

We are the ones to continue to walk in disobedience; sin. We are the ones to tell you that we like the beatings we are getting. So because of all of this and more, you have to leave the Black Man to their own condemnation; sins.

I tried and failed because she tied me and now she's dead, and like I've told you; I will never ever forgive her for what she has done to me. She broke me Lovey, she broke me come on now.

She did all to take you from me and I will never ever without end forgive her for this. Yes I know these words are echoed loud and clear in the universe and in hell, especially hell but this is the way it has to be and must be. You do not hurt people and or anyone that has done nothing to hurt you. You do not hurt people because someone tell you to and or pay you to do so. What evil did that person do you, for you to retaliate with evil like this? Hence no obeah man or woman, voodoo priest and priestess, shaman, witch or warlock and or what have you that seek the dead and evil spirits to hurt another human being or animal including spirit must ever have a place in our kingdom more than forever ever Good God and Allelujah without end. Absolutely none is permitted under any circumstances. You gave us good sight, hence keep your sight good and clean forever ever without end come on now.

You cannot destroy someone that has done you no wrong come on now. Hence I've told you Good God and Allelujah, I will never ever save anyone that is wicked and evil if I am the saving grace of humanity. They did wrong, so why should I save them from the wrongs they knowingly and willingly do.

And don't you dare tell me about judge not lest though be judged before I go ballistic on you.

Why the hell should good be the sacrifice of and for evil?

You did not tell any of us to go out and do evil, we choose to do evil; hence we chose evil over you. **TRUTH IS EVERLASTING LIFE AND INSTEAD OF LIVING BY TRUTH WE LIVE BY LIES AND DIE.**

Did I not tell you I don't want death to take me?
Did I not tell you I want you to take me?

I do not need to see the smile of death, I need to see and have the good and true life you ordained and commissioned for me and you come on now. I need to see and have your good and true life come on now. No one was to die. We were to walk to you in flesh and spirit but because of sin, flesh and spirit has become separated; cannot walk back to you whole.

Yes it's sad we cannot walk to you whole, but one day things will be renewed where there will be no sin and evil on earth or anywhere for that matter including the universe. **<u>The later, hell and death will pass away never ever to return to earth or anywhere in the universe.</u>**

We need this Lovey, so truly secure the children; our children and people and heal us so that we do not see, live or feel pain and death anymore.

Remember you showed me the names in Your Book of Life, so you trust me that much. So if you trust me to do this, then help me to truly help you in a good and true way. You cannot walk away from us; your good and true people because we need you.

You can no longer let death reach you.
You can no longer let death trick and deceive us.

You can no longer stand aside and look; watch as we die of need and want come on now.

You can no longer let wicked and evil people mess up and screw up our children. This is wrong.

The trend of evil cannot continue. Death lost in 2013 and no matter how death (Satan) transferred his power to a human (Jay Z); Nimrod must go down in hell with him because the King lost.

Satan lost so Satan's children including the churches of the globe must go down in hell, and every clergy member that sell humanity; humans' death must go down to hell with him. Come on now.

*Every government official that pays death by sacrificing their children on the battlefield of Death (Aries) must go down to hell and die. This is the law and you know this, hence Mother Earth must devour many lands that are above the sea (ground). Remember the law of death specifically states; "THE WAGES OF SIN IS DEATH, BUT TRUTH IS LIFE EVERLASTING AND OR ETERNAL." So because of this, you must adhere to the law of death and let him collect his and her pay. **HUMANS NOT YOU WERE THE ONES TO IGNORE THIS IMPORTANT FACT. THEY WERE THE ONES TO BUY INTO THE JESUS LIE.***

Hence I've told you time and time again to complete the separation of lands. Good can no longer live amongst evil because good need to live. We need to be at peace, true peace and it's not right for wicked and evil people to take you from us. Nor is it fair and just for wicked and evil people to take us with them to hell.

We want and need to live and you are hindering us from living. When you do this, you cannot blame us from turning against you because you are willingly and knowingly keeping us in sin. You are going against our good and true will hence you of yourself is sinning; doing wrong. You cannot go against the good and true will of your people and turn around and say YOU LOVE US SO.

This is bullshit on your part. You are the one telling us that you do not want good for yourself nor do you want good and truth for your people. <u>**You as a God cannot want what Death and or the Devil and or Satan has. What's theirs is theirs. You are the one to not secure your good and true people in a proper way.**</u> I've told you I want and need impenetrable foundations and frameworks with you so that when the Devil tries to penetrate us he can never ever do it again. <u>This impenetrable frameworks and foundations I more than need and want for our good and true people as well.</u> We know you and the full truth, so He or She cannot rock us or even come near to us. <u>We should now have evil repellant around us at all times.</u> The spacing should be more than infinite and indefinite forever ever *without end. Therefore evil and or sin and or wickedness can never reach us ever again.*

You have someone that has good and true will of you and for you but you don't have it for me or your good and true people, and I cannot talk to you anymore about this.

IF FATHER DOES NOT LISTEN, HOW THE HELL ARE YOU EXPECTING YOUR CHILDREN TO LISTEN? This cannot work because MANY OF US LEARN WHAT WE SEE OUR PARENTS DO. Come on now. So if you are cold and heartless then we will become cold and heartless also come on now.

If you have not charity and true love, we will come to have not charity and true love come on now.

I learn from you, so if you teach wrong, will I not teach and do wrongs also?

Yes there is more but I am going to leave things like this on this day and close this book. Yes I know she wants me to go to New York, but in truth Good God, I truly don't want to but yet I need to. Yes America is going to fall and your children have to get out, but why did they not listen to Marcus Mosiah Garvey?

Why did we forget Israel and Judah?

EVIL NEEDED ISRAEL AND JUDAH TO FAIL AND MODERN DAY ISRAEL (AMERICA) AND JUDAH (JAMAICA) FAILED. THEY BOTH SUPPORT THE DEVIL AND LOOK AT THEIR ECONOMY.

They (America, the United States of America) failed to realize that THEY HAD LIFE; YOUR GOOD AND TRUE LIFE (SPIRITUAL LIFE) WHICH IS THE UPRIGHT EYE IN TRIANGLE ON THEIR BANK NOTE. <u>*They claimed life; you; your spiritual life Good God and Allelujah in the living.*</u> THIS LIFE WAS WHAT SATAN WANTED. THIS IS WHAT THE DEVIL IS LOOKING FOR AND CAN'T GET. <u>SO IN DOING SO, HE SATAN HAD TO MAKE AMERICA, THE UNITED STATES OF AMERICA CRUMBLE.</u> SATAN HAD TO DESTROY THEIR ECONOMY. HE HAD TO MAKE THEM FIGHT; KILL TO THE BITTER END AND THEY DID KILL AND FIGHT; DESTROYED THEIR LAND. <u>THIS IS WHY WHEN DEATH TALKS</u>

ABOUT SIN, DEATH TALKS ABOUT THE UNITED STATES OF AMERICA. DEATH CAPTURED THE LAND AND PEOPLE AND NOW THE NAMES OF AMERICANS ARE ENGRAINED IN THE BOOK OF DEATH INDEFINITELY. AMERICA (THE UNITED STATES OF AMERICA) DID VIOLATE LIFE. THEY KILLED LIFE AND STILL KILLING LIFE. SATAN'S CHILDREN AND PEOPLE MOCK LIFE HENCE THE MANY HUMAN AND ANIMAL SACRIFICES THAT THEY DO INCLUDING THE LAW AND LAWS THEY WRITE TO KEEP THE POOR CAPTIVE WHILST THE WICKED AND EVIL, MANIPULATE AND FIND NEW WAYS AND MEANS TO STAY RICH AND KILL. SO BECAUSE OF THIS AND MORE AMERICA, THE UNITED STATES OF AMERICA MUST FALL; IS ORDAINED TO FALL; CRUMBLE.

- WHILE THE DEVIL WAS FLOURISHING THEY WERE SINKING SELF IN SIN, HENCE THEIR NATIONAL DEBT NONE CAN TRULY REPAY.

- While the devil was flourishing; they (America) killed and still kills whilst plunging land and people further into the darkness and depths of hell.

- *While the devil was flourishing, they (America) were expanding their hell hole in hell.*
- *While the devil was flourishing, they (America) were too busy racking up more time in hell for their land and people and still doing it; racking up more time in hell as I write.*

- *While the devil was flourishing, they (America) are too busy embroidering and securing the names of their people in hell.*

- *Until this day they cannot see this, hence unclean went to unclean and further sank Judah (Jamaica) into hell.*

Now the devil wants to go to Kenya to plunge that land (AFRICAN LAND AND LANDS) further into hell. Good God you cannot let this happen because I came to you with goodness and truth for this land (Kenya). It was a Kenyan that secured a home for me and my children to lay our heads, and I asked you, begged you for goodness for Kenya and you cannot let this demon that turned against you go to Kenya to destroy the land and people. I truly do not care if he has Kenyan roots, you cannot allow him passage in this land. I refuse him entry into this land and you have to do the same. Remember Mama Africa is tired. Hence the bullshit that is happening in Africa must stop. I will not allow anyone to go into this land and further destroy it. <u>MAMA AFRICA DOES NOT DESERVE WHAT SHE'S</u>

<u>GETTING FROM HER UNGRATEFUL AND DISGRACEFUL INCLUDING DECEITFUL OWN.</u>

These people claim African Lineage but yet destroy Africa and disgrace Africa each and every day. They've become so valueless that anyone can come into Africa and destroy it; feed them shit about AFRICAN LINEAGE AND HISTORY AND THEY EAT IT UP AND SAY IT'S GOOD FOOD.

<u>**Tell me, how the hell can you say you are an AFRICAN; THE ORIGINAL PEOPLE OF CREATION, AND DON'T EVEN KNOW YOUR OWN DAMN ROOTS AND CULTURE; HISTORY?**</u>

HOW THE HELL CAN ANY OF THEM SAY THEY ARE AFRICANS AND BUY INTO THE BULLSHIT OF RELIGION? SHOULD THEY AS AFRICANS NOT TEACH THE GLOBE, ALL OF HUMANITY ABOUT YOU GOOD GOD AND

ALLELUJAH? SHOULD THEY NOT BE THE ONES TO TEACH HUMANITY ABOUT AFRICAN ROOTS AND CULTURE?

SHOULD THEY AS AFRICANS NOT SET THE TREND FOR TRUTH AND CLEANLINESS? AFTERALL THEY CLAIM TO BE FROM THE BEGINNING OF TIME, AND CIVILIZATION BEGAN IN AFRICA.

WELL I SAY BLEEP THEM BECAUSE THEY'RE A BLEEPING DISGRACE UNTO THE HUMAN RACE. A BUNCH OF BLEEPING TURN COATS AND SELL OUTS, HENCE I KNOW MY ROOTS AND CULTURE INCLUDING CREATION.

IF THEY WERE AFRICANS, THEY WOULD KNOW THE TRUTH, TEACH THE TRUTH, LIVE BY THE TRUTH AND NOT LIES.

I do not need the filth and lies of man; so called Africans because I have more than the truth of Him Good God and Allelujah.

So bleep Man Kind and their bullshit lies and books.

You ordained him to bring the National Debt of the United States of America down, **and instead of securing the UPRIGHT EYE IN TRIANGLE HE DESTROYED IT.** So yes Jay Z must take him down because he did wine and dine; danced with the devil. He did side with the devil against you Good God; so what say him when America is destroyed? The devil had to destroy America because they (the United States of America) had life. **Marcus Mosiah Garvey did try to tell them this. HE WAS TRYING TO PREPARE THEM FOR THIS DAY; THE DAY WHEN AMERICA WOULD FALL DUE TO SINS, BUT THEY DID NOT TRUST HIM NOR DID THEY BELIEVE HIM. NOW MILLIONS IN AMERICA IS GOING TO LOSE IT ALL.** All their billionaires and millionaires that worship and bow down to Satan must now bow down to Jay-Z. Satan trusted him over them; hence Satan transferred his power to him (Jay Z) not the land. So Satan screwed them; the land of America; United States of America. America hath not power, Jay Z has. This is how I saw it and this is how I am relating it back to you. So Nimrod must take control not just in America. He must take the seat and or the throne of England. He is now the new King because Satan gave him the power to do so. Yes the family of King James; the monarchy of England fall under the Free Mason and or Illuminati Order, and because of this power transfer, he Jay Z can tell the Queen of England to vacate the throne because she's no longer queen; he is king. *And if you dispute this, then refer to Revelations because it's all there for you to read. The Queen of England no longer has power, Jay Z does.*

America, the United States of America had spiritual life and none knew this!!

Lovey, the UPRIGHT EYE IN TRIANGLE IS YOUR LIFE, ANYONE THAT HAS THIS, THE UPRIGHT EYE IN TRIANGLE IS GUARANTEED A PLACE WITH YOU AND AMERICA, THE UNITED STATES OF AMERICA HAD THIS AND LOST IT BECAUSE OF STUPIDITY.

HENCE LIFE CAME TO LIFE AND LIFE REJECTED LIFE. (Marcus Mosiah Garvey)

Thus no one can say you did not try because you did try. America trusted the devil over you that's all.

Michelle and Michelle Jean

Good God let me truly ask you something because this concerns me so much.

Tell me something, how are we going to live in Canada shortly? I am looking for a one bedroom apartment and my head is beginning to hurt me because I can't afford it.

I can't afford a one bedroom unit by myself. When did rent become so expensive that as human beings you cannot afford to live?

My head hurts looking at the price of these units. Now I understand and over stand why my second child is stressing because insurance premiums for him his over $700.00 per month. He wants to buy a car and he can't because he's basically working to pay insurance. How can anyone live with insurance being so high, rent being so high and food being so high?

So tell me now, if the simple person is bankrupt financially how can they live? Are the haves of society not causing them undue stress and pain?

No one can afford to live living on minimum wage. Something have to give because the way I see it, the rich and or one percent care not for the have nots; those that are struggling to get by. All he does is put more pressure on the struggling few and many. So tell me where is the fairness in this global society?

Now I comprehend and more than over stand the homelessness of LA. Greed is the basis of it all. The rich gain while the poor go down.

The rich man sees not the struggles of the poor man because the poor man is not his or her concern; their pocket book is.

So Lovey, what am I to do now knowing that I cannot afford to be on my own?

How are you going to help me financially to get by because I truly cannot get over just how expensive rent is, and I truly do not want to go live in a basement apartment? I cannot live in someone's home or room. It's just too hard for me, but yet I am trapped in an apartment that I need to get out of. I truly need to be on my own without my children. Yes they are going to have to face the battlefield on their own because none listened to me, but it's their doing and not mine. So in all I do, I have to find a way to make it instead of relying on you to open good doors for me. Like I've said, I've tried but it's not me failing you, it's you failing me. You are not opening good and true doors for me to go through. So yes, I have to leave things as is until I can find my true way by myself. **Yes it hurts to see the**

BATTLEFIELD OF LIFE BUT WHAT CAN I DO? THIS IS THE REALITY OF MAN. MANY ARE GOING TO BE HOMELESS REAL SOON IN TORONTO JUST LIKE IN LA. THERE IS NO AFFORDABLE HOUSING FOR PEOPLE THAT ARE SICKLY AND LIVING ON A FIXED INCOME LIKE ME AND THIS IS MORE THAN SAD; SHAMEFUL. <u>Hence the rich man will become like the poor man begging for bread in the streets.</u>

Many corporations are going to collapse for the few; 1% and rightfully so. They did not think of their unjust and unfair ways.

Scary and sad but this is what livity, the livity of man; human's have become.

If you cannot afford food and shelter, you will be left on the streets. I also have to think of the winter months on the streets. It's not like Canada has tropical climate, it has climate that are cold and sometimes brutal. Hence many people are going to die here also, because soon the job market will become scarcer and what then when it comes to food and shelter? <u>**Many black families**</u>

will be without a home and it's not like many can go back home. Many Caribbean Islands are going to face hardships due to their sins and corrupt ways.

Many will be homeless and the Government of Canada is not prepared for this massive homelessness.

Lovey, nothing is affordable anymore ,so what is man left to do?

What are your people left to do?

Hence I echo my cries with you yet again. I don't want to be here because I know what's ahead for millions in this country, and what's ahead is so not pretty.

Michelle and Michelle Jean

OTHER BOOKS BY MICHELLE JEAN

Blackman Redemption – The Fall of Michelle Jean
Blackman Redemption – After the Fall Apology
Blackman Redemption – World Cry – Christine Lewis
Blackman Redemption
Blackman Redemption – The Rise and Fall of Jamaica
Blackman Redemption – The War of Israel
Blackman Redemption – The Way I Speak to God
Blackman Redemption – A Little Talk With Man
Blackman Redemption – The Den of Thieves
Blackman Redemption – The Death of Jamaica
Blackman Redemption – Happy Mother's Day
Blackman Redemption – The Death of Faith
Blackman Redemption – The War of Religion
Blackman Redemption – The Death of Russia
Blackman Redemption – The Truth
Blackman Redemption – Spiritual War
Blackman Redemption – The Youths
Blackman Redemption – Black Man Where Is Your God?

The New Book of Life
The New Book of Life – A Cry For The Children
The New Book of Life – Judgement
The New Book of Life – Love Bound
The New Book of Life – Me
The New Book of Life – Life

Just One of Those Days
Book Two – Just One of Those Days
Just One of Those Days – Book Three The Way I Feel
Just One of Those Days – Book Four

The Days I Am Weak
Crazy Thoughts – My Book of Sin

Broken
Ode to Mr. Dean Fraser

A Little Little Talk
A Little Little Talk – Book Two

Prayers
My Collective
A Little Talk/A Time For Fun and Play
Simple Poems
Behind The Scars
Songs of Praise And Love

Love Bound
Love Bound – Book Two

Dedication Unto My Kids
More Talk
Saving America From A Woman's Perspective
My Collective the Other Side of Me
My Collective the Dark Side of Me
A Blessed Day
Lose To Win
My Doubtful Days – Book One

My Little Talk With God
My Little Talk With God – Book Two

A Different Mood and World – Thinking

My Nagging Day
My Nagging Day – Book Two
Friday September 13, 2013
My True Love
It Would Be You

My Day

A Little Advice – Talk
1313, 2032, 2132 – The End of Man
Tata

MICHELLE'S BOOK BLOG – BOOKS 1 – 20

My Problem Day
A Better Way
Stay – Adultery and the Weight of Sin – Cleanliness Message

Let's Talk
Lonely Days – Foundation
A Little Talk With Jamaica – As Long As I Live
Instructions For Death
My Lonely Thoughts
My Lonely Thoughts – Book Two
My Morning Talks – Prayers With God
What A Mess
My Little Book
A Little Word With You
My First Trip of 2015
Black Mother – Mama Africa
Islamic Thought
My California Trip January 2015
My True Devotion by Michelle – Michelle Jean
My Many Questions To God
My Talk
My Talk Book Two
My Talk Book Three – The Rise of Michelle Jean